REAL

A CONVERSATION FROM MY HEART TO YOURS

TALK

ISBN 978-0-692-15602-5

This title is available as a BFF Publishing House Ebook.

Request for information should be addressed to:

praytheimpossible@gmail.com

Cover Design: Thomas Teel

BFF Publishing House is a Limited Liability Corporation dedicated wholly to the appreciation and publication of children and adults for the advancement of diversification in literature.

For more information on publishing contact
Antionette Mutcherson at
bff@bffpublishinghouse.com

Website: bffpublishinghouse.com

Published in the United States by BFF Publishing House
Tallahassee, Florida First Edition, 2018

DEDICATION

I dedicate this book to the loves of my life; my mother, father, brother, Nana, my niece and to the rest of my family members. Thank you for always supporting me in every endeavor of my life. Thank you for always being there to celebrate every achievement in my life. I know writing this book may have come as a surprise, but I hope that I've made you all proud.

To my support system; my friends, besties, my spiritual sistahs, line sisters, church family and those who God has sent along the way to play a role in my life's journey. Thank you all for always encouraging me, supporting me, praying for me, being a listening ear, but most importantly for allowing me to pour into your spirits. I couldn't have asked for a better group of people to experience life with.

To my co-friends (co-workers) thank you for being open to speak with me about God in the workplace. I never knew that my morning walk-bys past your desks would turn into conversations that magnify the Lord. Our office conversations have helped me to realize that I am a walking testimony and the following conversations have turned into my purpose.

NB, I thank God for using you to be a part of my spiritual journey and growth to becoming a woman of God. Thank you for inspiring me. A to the M-E-N.

ACKNOWLEDGMENT

I want to acknowledge the God I serve. My Jesus year has definitely been the hardest year of my life thus far, and it is certainly one for the books, literally. I am truly humbled to be your anointed and chosen vessel to spread your word. I pray that this book of conversations touches the heart of everyone who reads this book. I realized it was never about me.

I want to acknowledge my Sistah from another Mistah, Kharisma. From the bottom of my heart thank you. If you had never extended the invitation to visit The House of The Lord Church in Englewood, New Jersey I know that I would not be the woman of God that I am today.

I want to acknowledge my Pastor Evangelist Dawnique Daughtry. Pastor, thank you for pouring into my life for the past eleven years. Thank you for your words that have helped to mold and shape me. Thank you for being my Pastor that helped to nurture my relationship with God. I am forever grateful to be a member of The House of the Lord under your leadership.

I want to acknowledge Minister Lorenzo and Sister Sarah Daughtry-Chambers. If you had not spoken a prophetic word over my life about writing a book about my transformation, I do not believe that it would have come to fruition. Thank you for speaking a word that allowed my purpose to G.L.O.W.

I want to acknowledge the Teels. Thank you for our Sunday night "Real Talk" conversations. Thank you for the picturesque image that expresses what a conversation from my heart to yours looks like. Our conversations allowed me to pour my heart out, and the picturesque image that was created for the cover mirrors what a conversation from my heart to yours looks like.

TABLE OF CONTENTS

INTRODUCTION

REAL TALK is a conversation between men and women of God and believers in Jesus Christ about the ups, downs, twists, turns, the highs and lows of life. It's an open conversation from one heart to another featuring testimonies that exemplify the work that God has done through some people and for some people. These conversations help to build faith, encouragement, hope, and healing to overcome situations that life throws our way.

I wrote this book based on a word spoken over me by my Minister and his wife. They prophesied that I would write a book about my transformation. I did not think that I would be writing a devotional book. The devotional book manifested itself after my Pastor asked me to deliver a Sunday message in December 2017. After my Sunday word, I found myself looking for inspiration, and I began writing in a journal about my life experiences that people can relate to. One day I remembered that prophecy, and with the grace of God, you are holding thirty devotionals authored with love and God's divine light.

My life is a walking testimony. Whether I am giving a testimony during church, advising a friend, or encouraging someone who was sent along my path, I find myself having a conversation about what I've experienced and how God helped me get through it.

I believe that God is using me as His vessel to spread a word to people in this generation who are seeking Him, who want to strengthen their relationship with Him, whose faith is shakable, or those who need to witness the power of God showing up in the lives of others. I am a witness to the power of faith, and in this devotional, I want to encourage you through Biblical references and life experiences on your journey with faith. Let's have a real conversation.

REAL TALK

CONVERSATION 1

God Will Show Up and Show Out

"For with God nothing will be impossible." Luke 1:37 NKJV

Are you currently experiencing a situation that seems impossible? Do you think to yourself how am I going to work this out? Or better yet do you believe that the circumstance will not turn around in your favor? What you are experiencing is not meant for you to figure it. The situation is intended for you to let God do what only God can do and watch God show up and show out in your life.

Would you believe that I did not grow up attending church regularly nor did I grow up having a relationship with God? It is true. It was not until 2007 when my sistah from another Mistah invited me to attend her church with her that I began going faithfully. I remember my very first experience with God in 2008 that changed my life. He showed up and showed out on my behalf. A college colleague of mine helped me to get a job as a Sales Assistant working for an event planning magazine that she too worked for. One day she and I were having a regular conversation, and I mentioned to her about a situation I had just encountered after filing my taxes. At 23 years old, while working for the first time in my career, I owed the IRS $3,000.00. My employer at the time did not take taxes out of my check, and I was unaware that I needed to set money aside for taxes to pay at the end of the year. I did not know what I was going to do or where I was going to get the money from to pay the taxes.

After all, at that time I was making under 30k a year

in my new position, I paid $700 a month to Sallie Mae, and I was living off of $100 after expenses until my next paycheck. The next day, my colleague pulled me into the kitchen and handed me an envelope and told me not to worry about paying her back. As a young woman of God, she informed me that the Lord spoke to her after our conversation. She told me, "Jesus died on the cross for my sins, and there is no way that I could ever repay Him. The only thing that I can do is to help someone else." The envelope that she handed me was filled with the money that I needed to pay my taxes. She was the vessel, through her GOD SHOWED UP AND SHOWED OUT!

What looked impossible to me, God made possible. All it took was a conversation for God to use her to be the answer to "where am I going to get the money from?" to bless me. I will always remember 4/16/2008 for the rest of my life. That was the day I experienced God in my life. I believe that He uses situations that seem hopeless to make you trust that He will show up and show out. I hope my testimony will help you to believe that no matter what you are going through, God will show up and show out in your life.

Heart to Heart

Are you currently experiencing a situation that
seems impossible to conquer?
Have you witnessed God show up in your life before?
With God, did you conquer that
"impossible" situation?

_____

_____

_____

_____

_____

_____

_____

_____

_____

_____

_____

_____

_____

_____

_____

_____

_____

_____

_____

_____

CONVERSATION 2

Are You Putting God First or Just Waiting to See Your Answered Prayers?

"But seek first the kingdom of God and His righteousness and all these things shall be added to you." Matthew 6: 33 NKJV

When you wake up in the morning are you checking your phone notifications first or are you thanking God for waking you up before doing anything else? Are you watching the news first or are you having a conversation with God to start your day? Are you going about your day as usual, waiting and expecting God to answer your prayers without putting Him first? Have you ever thought that God is waiting to give you what you are praying for? Maybe God is waiting for you to put Him first.

Perhaps He needs to prune you of your old habits and ways of thinking. Perhaps He needs to change your heart. Maybe He wants to see if you will genuinely cast all your cares and worries upon Him. Maybe God is taking His time to get you ready for the new thing that He has for you. Maybe God is shaping and molding you to become the person He's ordained you to be. Maybe it is the renewed version of yourself that God wants you to become who will be ready to handle and receive the blessings that He has for you. The key to getting all that you pray for is to put God first then everything will be added to your life.

Maybe you are waiting for God to bless you with a financial breakthrough. You may feel as though you can't seem to catch a break. You are always worried about your finances instead of trusting God to make a way with the money that you already have. You pray for a pay raise at work and another year goes by without an increase. Or maybe someone asks to borrow money from you, and you tell them you do not have the money even though you do. Or maybe you have not reached a place in your spiritual walk where you are ready and willing to tithe. You feel that you will not have enough money to pay your bills or spend it on the things that you want. After crying out to the Lord and deciding to put Him first, you realize that God was allowing this financial drought. God revealed to you that you were putting your worries about your finances first instead of putting Him first. He wanted to show you that to receive, your heart must be willing to give first. He showed you that He wanted to change your heart from being selfish to being generous. He wanted to see if you had the FAITH to TRUST Him. He wanted to know if you would be a blessing to someone. He wanted to see if your heart was willing to let go of everything that you have prayed for.

Maybe you are waiting for God to send you the man or woman you've been praying for. You have gone on hundreds of dates, talked to men or women who you thought were "the one," and it turned out that they were not. After months or years of dealing with this, you finally realize that you cannot do it anymore in your own strength. You decide to reflect and spend quality time with God. After disappointments and witnessing your friends enter into relationships, it dawns on you that God may be using these situations to draw you closer to Him. How could you pray to be in a relationship with someone, when the most important relationship that you will ever have was non-existent? If you do not have a relationship with God, and there is no greater love than one with God, how could you seriously manage a relationship with your dream man or woman? By getting closer to God, you invite Him to reveal things about you that you may need to change. When the time is right, He will also reveal to you why He allowed you to experience the things that you went through.

Most of the time we become impatient because we want to receive the answered prayer on our time and not trust in God's time. God's time is different from our time. 2 Peter 3:8 NLT states, "A day is like a thousand years to the Lord, and a thousand years is like a day." While we are waiting, we are given tests that force us to change our ways, trust and depend on God and put Him first. The pruning, changing your thoughts and attitude are all a part of the process of receiving your answered prayer.

During this process, you may have learned how to forgive those who have hurt you. Maybe you have learned that communication is critical. Maybe you have learned not to put your expectations in man but to place them in God instead. Maybe you have learned what real love is because you have strengthened your relationship with God. Maybe you have learned how to worship and praise God. Maybe you have learned to put God first and not the materialistic "gods" that you were idolizing. Whatever it may be, God needed time to change, mold, and shape you into the person who is ready to receive what you have been praying for. You have to trust God, spend time with God, and put Him first so that He can give you everything that you have been praying for.

Heart to Heart

What is the first thing you do when you wake up
each morning?
Are you thanking God first or do you check your phone
before starting your day?
What are some ways you can start putting God first
in your life?

_____

_____

_____

_____

_____

_____

_____

_____

_____

_____

_____

_____

_____

_____

_____

_____

_____

_____

CONVERSATION 3

Detach From Your Wants and Attach To Your Needs

"Father, if you are willing, please take this cup of suffering away from me. Yet I want your will to be done, not mine." Luke 22: 42 NLT

What are some of the things that you have prayed for that you desperately want to the point that you have become obsessive? Is it a new job? A new car? A house? Children? Marriage? What happens when God doesn't give you what you want? Do you get angry? Depressed? Upset? Discouraged? I can admit that I have felt these emotions on numerous occasions. I did not understand why God wasn't blessing me with what I wanted. I thought to myself, "I attend church regularly, pay tithes and offerings, pray for other people and yet I watch God answer the prayers of others. I asked myself, "What was I doing wrong?" Absolutely nothing is what I concluded. Eventually, I realized that I had been holding on to my wants and was not being open to receive what I needed from God.

It wasn't until I decided to participate in an *Oprah & Deepak's 21-Day Meditation Experience* that it finally clicked. Essentially this meditation was about being open to receive what the universe, as Oprah and Deepak states, has for you. The Meditation felt more like a twenty one day transformation of letting go of self and becoming more aware of the infinite possibilities that the universe has to offer. At the end of the 21-day meditation, I had an AHA moment. I realized that what I wanted wasn't what I needed. That realization became my food for thought.

We can become so obsessed with what we want that we close God into a confined box of doing things in a specific way that we envision. Sometimes our desires are not aligned with the will that God has for us. That is why God does not bless us with our desires because He wants us to let go and be open to all that He has in store for us. God wants us to ask for things that are in alignment with His will; simultaneously He does not want us to become so consumed with our wants that we are not open to what He has planned for us. God gives us what we want but not always in the way we expect it; however, it is always in a way that we need it.

Subsequently, that relationship that you have been praying to God about, if you have a person in mind, you must be willing to detach that specific person from your prayer and vision and thank God for "the man or woman" that God has for you. That position that you desperately desire, start praising God in advance for the promotion that is going to advance you and positively change the trajectory of your career in ways that you cannot imagine. The car that you are dreaming about, begin to thank God in advance for the reliable transportation that He is going to provide. Be open to receive the blessings that God has for you because it is going to blow your mind what God desires to give you.

Heart to Heart

Have you become obsessed with what you are praying for?
Are you focused more on the answered prayer than what
God has in store for you?
Are you open for God to give you your wants the way
He sees fit?

_____

_____

_____

_____

_____

_____

_____

_____

_____

_____

_____

_____

_____

_____

_____

_____

_____

_____

_____

_____

CONVERSATION 4

How Big Is Your Faith?

"Truly I tell you, if you have faith as small as a mustard seed, you can say to this mountain 'move from here to there, and it will move. Nothing will be impossible for you." Matthew 17: 20 NIV

Everyone has faith on the inside. Some have unleashed that faith while others have left it untapped. God has given everyone faith the size of a mustard seed. A mustard seed is small in size, but when planted it produces a large plant. Do you see how something so little can be so powerful? Imagine if your faith was extraordinarily enormous, what do you think the outcome would be? Have patience with yourself. It takes time to increase your faith. Nevertheless, the good thing about God is that we do not need great faith to move mountains.

For example, I use mustard seed size faith for simple everyday things like when I am waiting for the bus to go to work. As a New Jersey native, I travel by public transportation to work in New York City 5 days a week. Living the city life gets hectic even as a seasoned traveler, I lean on God to get me through my commute. I pray to God that the bus is not standing room only. There have been plenty of days God has answered that prayer because the good Lord knows standing on the bus commuting in traffic is the worst.

Let me tell you about MY EXTRAORDINARILY BIG FAITH! It took years to build my big faith, but it happened. I have seen God work miracles in my life and I am compelled to believe that it is in part due to my faith. I can remember when a good friend of mine told me about her prayer jar. She explained to me how she used a mason jar from her kitchen and wrote down prayers for people and then placed the prayers in her jar. Sooner than later she said that her prayers were answered. I said to myself that is a fantastic idea. I decided to use a Talenti ice cream jar for mine. I wrote down prayers for family, friends and myself. I made sure to write the date on the paper with my prayer requests before placing my prayers in the jar. When one of my prayers were answered, I instantly remembered my prayer jar and searched for the piece of paper in which I had written down that specific prayer that God answered. Sometimes it took months or even a year before God responded to my prayer, but the time frame did not matter because I believed that God was going to answer my prayers.

Another way that I exercise my BIG FAITH is through creating vision boards. Whatever my heart desire is I find pictures and words to put on the board that represents that desire. I keep my vision board in a place where I can see it every day to remind myself of what God is preparing to do through me and for me. Every time something on my board manifest I write down the date that God answered my prayer. 90% of my vision board had manifested in the same year of me creating the board. Big Faith starts with a mustard seed size of faith. My mustard seed size faith has developed into big faith, which has caused several mountains to move at Godspeed out of my life.

Heart to Heart

How big is your faith?
How are you exercising your faith?
What are some practical tools that you have implanted to
increase your faith?

_____

_____

_____

_____

_____

_____

_____

_____

_____

_____

_____

_____

_____

_____

_____

_____

_____

_____

CONVERSATION 5

Receive It with Thanks

"Since everything God created is good, we should not reject any of it but receive it with thanks." 1 Timothy 4: 4 NLT
"I will praise you, Lord, with all my heart; I will tell if all the marvelous things you have done." Psalm 9:1 NLT

Have you done a heart check lately? You are probably wondering what I mean by a heart check. I'm not talking about a heart check that occurs when you receive your annual check-up at the doctor's office. In this instance, I am speaking of spending time with yourself and doing a self-check of your mind, heart, and spirit. Is your heart hardened from past pains, disappointments, and struggles? Do you see the glass as half empty instead of half full? Are you always anticipating something negative to happen because life has handed you a bag of lemons? If your answer is yes to ALL or most of these questions, then it is time to do a heart check. Take a deep breath, look yourself in the mirror, and begin to reflect on why you may have become jaded.

The first step is to surrender to God and let Him into your heart. Ask God to create in you a clean and pure heart. Ask Him to remove all impurities that have caused your heart to harden. Seek God and ask Him for forgiveness of all the things that you have done that were not pleasing to Him. Learn to forgive those who have wronged you. Forgive yourself for the things you have done. Ask God to open and soften your heart. Ask God to renew your mind and transform your thoughts. These are some of the initial steps to take into consideration for your heart check. Remember that it is a process, so be mindful to ask God for these things every day. It is a daily transformation, do not be too hard on yourself. Do not expect your healing to happen overnight. Slowly but surely your outlook on what you used to view as negative will become positive.

In the latter part of 2015, my cousin gave me a gratitude journal, *A Daily Appreciation* by Brendan Nathan. In this journal, Brendan Nathan states, "gratitude is the appreciation for every moment in your life. It is a feeling of abundance. It is saying thank you to the universe for what you have right now." She goes on to instruct readers to write down two to five things that they are grateful for over the course of a year. By the end of 2016, I learned to be thankful for the good and the bad, as well, as the big and the small. So, guess what? My heart now overflows with the peace of God.

Being grateful for everything creates room in your heart for God to bless you with more. Learning to be grateful gives you a sense of peace that only God can provide you with. The next time someone hurts you, forgive him or her, instead of holding a grudge. The next time you find a parking spot after driving around for thirty minutes or so, be grateful. The next time someone stops and asks you for directions be thankful that you were able to help. The transformation process from a hardened heart and negative thoughts to a heart that is filled with gratitude with an optimistic outlook is a beautiful one. An attitude of gratitude and seeing the glass as half full instead of half empty will take you places that you have never imagined.

Heart to Heart

Has your heart hardened from past hurts and experiences?
Do you view the glass as half empty instead of half full?
What are some things that you are thankful for?

_____

_____

_____

_____

_____

_____

_____

_____

_____

_____

_____

_____

_____

_____

_____

_____

_____

_____

_____

_____

CONVERSATION 6

It Will...

"Remember your promise to me; it is my only hope. Your promise revives me; it comforts me in all my troubles." Psalms 119:49-50 NLT

Are there promises that God made to you last year? A few months ago? This week? Did He promise you Peace? Joy? Restoration? Love? Abundance? Whatever your IT is, before the promise can manifest, IT will move you, and IT will test you. When God speaks a promise over your life, be sure to know that an obstacle, test, and oppositions will appear beforehand. Your promise is far greater than any test that comes your way. The enemy comes to steal, kill and destroy, so be aware when you feel him creeping up on you. Find comfort in knowing that your promise is coming after you survive the devil's tricks, plot, and scheme.

The enemy is trying to distract you and wants to take your eyes off the promise that God has in store for you. Do not believe the lies of the enemy because he is a liar. God is not a man, and He cannot lie. Whatever He spoke over your life believe that it will come to pass. Whether the promise takes months or even a year, it will come to pass. It will come to pass because God's timing is different from our timing.

While you are waiting for your promise, remember to put your hope in God's word. Use His promise to move you to a place of acting as if you already have received IT. Let it drive you to a deeper place in your faith. James 1:3-4 NLT states, "For you know that when your faith is tested, your endurance has a chance to grow." The moment you receive your promise, you will appreciate that IT moved you and that IT tested you. God saw you through, and He is pleased that you did not throw in the towel. It's a good thing you did not give up. You could have missed your promise because this could have been the promise that you have been praying for. This could be your promise that takes you to the next level in every area of your life.

Heart to Heart

Are there unfulfilled promises that God made to you?
Do you believe that those promises will be fulfilled?
How are you preparing for your promise(s)?

_____

_____

_____

_____

_____

_____

_____

_____

_____

_____

_____

_____

_____

_____

_____

_____

_____

_____

_____

CONVERSATION 7

Break the Cycle

"I am praying to you because I know that you will answer, O God. Bend down and listen as I pray." Psalms 17: 6 NLT

Are there experiences from your past that keep reoccurring in your present situations? Maybe you witnessed something in your childhood that has become a pattern in your adult life? Whatever the harmful habits, actions, or thoughts may be, you have the power through God to break the cycle. Did you grow up in a household where your parent(s) were not affectionate? Perhaps as an adult, you find yourself not showing affection to your significant other. Did you grow up in a single parent household and witnessed your parent struggling to make ends meet? As an adult, you find yourself in the same situation as your parent. Or maybe you weren't raised by either of your parents, and you grew up wondering what it felt like to have that family structure.

As you reflect on these childhood experiences, you realize that this has played a significant role in the person you have grown to become. Maybe you have grown into a person who does not know how to show affection or communicate effectively. Perhaps these experiences have left you feeling cold and not wanting to let anyone get close to you for fear of abandonment. Maybe these experiences left you angry and or bitter. Or perhaps the hurt little boy or hurt little girl is still living inside of you as an adult causing you to run away from adult problems.

Have you ever wondered why? By analyzing the situation, you may realize that your parent was not affectionate because their parent (your grandparent) was not affectionate either. It became a generational curse of non-affection and non-expression of emotions. Maybe growing up your parents did not set an example of what a healthy relationship should reflect. Again, perhaps they did not have an example of a healthy relationship because they too grew up in a broken home. Or now you realize that your single parent sacrificed continuing their education to settle for a job that did not pay well so that they could fill the void of your absentee parent. Or you concluded that your parents didn't raise you because they didn't know how to be a parent to you and wanted you to have a better life than they had. Or maybe the reason why you are running away from your problems is because you witnessed your parents running away from their issues instead of dealing with them head-on.

Regardless of what you may have experienced from past generational behaviors, habits, and actions it has influenced and shaped you into the person that you are today. Do not allow "generational curses" to affect how you see your future. Those situations can make or break you. You can either follow in their footsteps or chose to go the opposite way. The Bible states in Philippians 4:13 NLT "I can do all things through Christ who strengthens me." Talk to God. He's waiting to hear from you. If you feel that you are heading down the same path as the generations that came before you, ask for His supernatural strength to be the one to break the curse. Ask Him for His guidance to direct your path so that you can set an example for the generations to come.

If you did not grow up in a family that prayed with and for each other, it is not too late to start praying with and for your family. Up until now, you were not given an example of what a godly marriage requires, begin to read the Bible or marital devotionals that provide insight on what a godly husband and a godly wife looks like. If you are accustomed to running away from your problems take the time to confront the fear that keeps you running away. God may be trying to get your attention if you keep experiencing the same situation, habits, actions, and thoughts, over and over again. Be aware. Whatever the generational curse is, let it motivate you to break the cycle today. God has appointed you to be the generational curse breaker.

Heart to Heart

What are some family traits that have been passed down
from previous generations?
Can you identify a cycle that you are willing to break?
What are some steps that you can take to break the cycle(s)?

_____

_____

_____

_____

_____

_____

_____

_____

_____

_____

_____

_____

_____

_____

_____

_____

_____

_____

_____

_____

_____

_____

CONVERSATION 8

Pray the Impossible

"With men this is impossible, but with God all things are possible."
Matthew 19:26 NKJV

What is prayer? It is a solemn request for help or expression of thanks addressed to God; or an earnest request. What does impossible mean? It is the inability to occur, exist, or be done; very difficult to deal with. Are you currently facing a situation in life that seems impossible? Are you sick and think that you will never be healed? Are you depressed and believe that you will never see the light at the end of the tunnel? Are you single and think that you will be alone for the rest of your life? Are you in financial hardship because you have more bills than money at the end of each month? If so, I can also relate to situations that look as if it is they are impossible of turning around. There is a situation that my family and I have been dealing with for the past four years that seems impossible. The hardest part about praying for the impossible is to pray without ceasing even when the situation is going opposing what you are praying for. What most people fail to realize is that God is with us along our journey as we experience these difficulties. God allows these seemingly impossible situations to occur so that He can show us that He is able to turn the impossible to possible.

When facing moments or a season of difficulty your prayer is a solemn request to God asking for His help. This past year I have witnessed God turning my family situation around. I have been praying the impossible nearly every day, and slowly but surely, I am witnessing God breakthrough this situation that seems impossible.

There were times where my family and I wanted to give up because the circumstances looked like it was not turning in our favor. Going through life facing challenges, situations, and trials that seem to be impossible would make anyone want to throw in the towel to give up. Honestly, we all have a breaking point. With prayers from our Pastor, church family, and friends I decided that instead of worrying about the situation, I am going to continue to pray for everyone who is involved in the situation. It is times like this that I am reminded that God is more significant than our problems and He is indeed turning things around in our favor.

Each day I remind myself that God wants us to cast all our cares and worries unto Him because He cares for us. He knows that we are not able to handle what we are going through WITHOUT HIM! He's looking for us to pray and communicate with Him to help us overcome what seems far-fetched. God instructs us in Mark 11:23-24 NLT "But you must really believe it will happen and have no doubt in your heart. I tell you, you can pray for anything, and if you believe that you have received it, it will be yours." Whatever you are praying for, begin visualizing in your mind as though God has already manifested it. Visualize yourself healed, full of joy, in a healthy relationship, or financially blessed. He wants you to trust and believe that He can do it.

I want to encourage you that whatever you are facing the help you need is only possible with God. He wants you to have the faith that He can turn around what seems impossible in your life. God is a way maker. God performs wonders and miracles every day. The request for help from God will conquer what at first seems unable to be done. Only God can handle what is challenging for you to deal with. What's impossible with man, is possible with God.

Heart to Heart

Are you in the midst of an "impossible" situation?
Is your faith wavering because your situation looks like it will
not turn around in your favor?
Do you believe that God can make the
impossible possible?

_____

_____

_____

_____

_____

_____

_____

_____

_____

_____

_____

_____

_____

_____

_____

_____

_____

_____

_____

_____

_____

_____

CONVERSATION 9

Don't Keep It To Yourself

"So faith comes from hearing, that is, hearing the good news about Christ." Romans 10:17 NLT

God created humans to be relational and compassionate. We were designed to help each other out especially when our sisters and brothers need help. Most importantly, we are to spread the good news of Jesus Christ. By guiding others to Christ, we introduce them to the most rewarding relationship that they could possibly obtain. Believers in Christ are at different stages in their walk and relationship with Him. Some believers did not grow up in church but believe in God because they know there's a higher being. However, they do not have a relationship with Him because some chains and strongholds are holding them back from entirely giving their lives to God. Then, there are the believers who attend church every Sunday, read the bible often, and pray to God daily. These are the believers who have a deep relationship with God, and because of that, they recognize His still small voice. These believers listen and apply God's guidance to their lives.

By engaging God, your faith continues to grow as you consistently seek and hear His word. My advice to the believer who is more mature in their spiritual walk with God is to share your testimony. Do not keep what you're going through or overcome to yourself. Romans 10:14 NLT it states, "and how can they hear about Him unless someone tells them." You may be further along on your spiritual journey to help the believer who does not know God the way you have grown to know Him. Perhaps a friend, family member, or a co-worker may believe in God but cannot understand how you continue to press on when you are going through your season of drought. What they do not know is that the light of God that is within you attracts you to them. God is drawing nonbelievers close to you because He is using what He's doing in your life as an example of what He could do for them in their lives.

It is essential to spread the good news of Jesus while you are going through trials and tribulations so that when you are victorious, both believers and nonbelievers in Christ will look at you and recognize that God's grace is still life changing. By witnessing your testimony, they will know that had it not been for God, you would have been defeated. They will see a change in you while you are in your season of abundance. Share your story. Whether you know it or not, we are all a walking testimony; especially if you have lived long enough to experience hurt, pain, joy, and happiness. God has given us the assignment to help someone get closer to Him through our testimonies. What a small price to pay! People may not know God for themselves, but they should know what God is doing for you and in you. Tell others of His great works and about the miracles that He has performed in your life. It just may not only save someone's life but, also their soul.

Heart to Heart

When you are going through a trial, do you keep it
to yourself?
Has someone ever shared their testimony with you and it
encouraged you?
Are you open to sharing your testimony with others?

_____

_____

_____

_____

_____

_____

_____

_____

_____

_____

_____

_____

_____

_____

_____

_____

_____

_____

_____

_____

CONVERSATION 10

Only God

"And the peace of God that surpasses all understanding will guard your hearts and minds in Jesus Christ." Philippians 4:7 NET

Shocked. Stunned. In disbelief. Confused. These are all initial feelings that sometimes overtake you when you have been blindsided by a situation that you never imagined would impact your life. Life may have been going exceptionally well, but it was only a matter of time before it is your turn to come off the mountaintop and into the valley. You immediately turn to God because after all, He is the only one who will get you out of your unexpected situation.

You begin to ponder on other traumatic experiences that you have faced throughout your life, and wonder how did I make it through that? How did I survive that? How am I able to reflect on past situations without feeling the pain from old wounds? Only God can bring us out of such trials, tests, and tribulations. This time around your reaction is different. For some reason in the midst of your storm, while you're in the middle of it, you feel a sense of peace that surpasses all understanding.

Only God can give you that kind of peace. He loves and cares for you that much. In the eye of the storm, you must realize that this situation is how God advances you to another level. At that moment, you know that this situation is working for your good. You now understand that you are experiencing God in a new way. Immediately you can reflect and see the good in your situation. As you face adversity, you are more relaxed than you have ever been before. Recognizing that God is God all by himself, you trust that He will turn the situation around in due time. You understand that the lesson that God is teaching you will bless you. You have solace in knowing that only God can and will see you through.

When I think about unexpected circumstances, I think about the Bible story of Job. How much faith he had in God is inspirational. God allowed the enemy to take away Job's prized possessions, his family and friends, and his riches. The enemy thought Job would curse and turn on God. Only God knew how faithful Job would be to Him. And it was only God who was able to give Job double in return for his troubles. When I reflect on this story, I am reassured that only God will grant us the peace that we need to overcome any and every situation. I know that it is only God that I can call on. It is only God who I put my trust and hope in. It is only God who will give me double for my trouble.

Heart to Heart

In times of trouble, do you turn to God or family/friends?
Are you spending time with God when you're in the valley?
Do you look at unexpected situations as an opportunity for
God to strengthen your faith?

_____

_____

_____

_____

_____

_____

_____

_____

_____

_____

_____

_____

_____

_____

_____

_____

_____

_____

_____

_____

CONVERSATION 11

Check Your Spiritual Files

"Now go, write it down on a tablet in their presence, inscribe it on a scroll, so that it might be preserved for a future time as an enduring witness." Isaiah 30:8 NLT

When you are going through what appears to be the worst times of your life, where do you turn for encouragement or comfort? During the trial are you seeking guidance from friends and family first or God and His word? In the earlier days of my Christian walk, my first reaction would be to turn to friends. Then as I matured in my faith, I realized the first person I should be turning to was God. He's the only one who can truly comfort me. As I seek God, I allow the Holy Spirit to direct my steps and guide me. I've been a member of my church for 11 years, and I make sure to take notes at every service. I cannot even begin to tell you how many notebooks I have with notes from my Pastor's sermons.

The sermons preached are ones of hope, courage, joy, expectancy, and comfort. Unfortunately, as life happens, I tend to forget about the notebooks. It's not until I am in the eye of the storm feeling lost, confused, and hopeless that I pray to God and ask Him for help. At that moment, the Holy Spirit leads me to my notebooks. As I scroll through the pages of my notebooks searching for a word, I realized that I'm checking my spiritual files. What are spiritual files? These are files that you can always check to reference God's word at any given moment. Sometimes sermons are not meant for you at that particular time that you hear it. The word may not apply to you at that moment because it is not your season.

REAL TALK

Writing Gods messages down allows you access to His instruction at a future date. There will come a time when the spoken word will be exactly what you need. It is essential to keep a spiritual file, whether it is for you or for someone that you know. These files will get you through the tough times when you feel all hope is lost. Maybe you do not have a spiritual file such as written notes from sermons, perhaps someone has sent you scriptures, or you have read devotionals, or seen some inspirational word on social media. In whatever form you receive it, begin to collect the word of God to create your spiritual file. These are the files that will get you through the next time you are in the valley.

Heart to Heart

When experiencing tough times, where do you find comfort
and encouragement?
Do you have a spiritual file?
Are there inspirations or sermons that you can
gather to create a spiritual file?

_____

_____

_____

_____

_____

_____

_____

_____

_____

_____

_____

_____

_____

_____

_____

_____

_____

_____

_____

CONVERSATION 12

Let Go...Draw Closer to God

"Do not remember the former things, nor consider the things of old."
Isaiah 43:18 NLT

Let go, words that are easy to say but hard to implement. How do you let go of things that have hurt you, let you down, disappointed you, or that have broken you? It is much easier to hold onto the anger, hurt, pain, and depression. Holding on to the past is not going to help you move forward, nor will it help in the healing process. Dwelling on the past is not suitable for your mental, emotional, physical, or spiritual state. You are allowing the enemy to steal your joy, peace, faith and positive thoughts. The enemy's purpose is to attack you at your weakest moment. Before you allow that to happen open yourself up to a... But God!

God is on your side fighting your battle, but He's waiting for you to let go and draw closer to Him. The only way we can draw closer to Him is by letting go and surrendering all to Him. The scripture tells us to forget the former things and not to remember (Isaiah 43:18). How do you even begin to etch these thoughts from your mind? The answer is by seeking God. Put God first and make Him the head of your life. Be intentional about seeking Him throughout the day and the night. Talk to God and express everything that is concerning you. Cast all of your cares and worries unto Him because He cares (Peter 5:7). This is one of many scriptures that I repeat to myself to center my thoughts. Perhaps try to find a scripture to memorize and to meditate on His word. Ask God to renew your mind and transform your thoughts. Ask God to give you His perfect peace and positive thoughts. Breathe. Ask God for His strength to help you control your thoughts. PRAY! PRAY! And PRAY some more.

Take time to fast from things that are distracting you. This could mean people, things, and places so that you can focus on God. Listen to gospel music. Remember to LET IT GO! The past is the past, and God is calling you to a new place. The new level where God is taking you, the hurt, disappointments, and anger are not welcomed. Let go of everything that is holding you back from drawing closer to Him. God will always provide you with the strength to let go as soon as you decide to draw closer to Him.

Heart to Heart

What are you holding onto that scares you to let go of?

What is it about your past that keeps you from moving forward on your spiritual journey?

Is the thing that you're holding onto from your past worth your relationship with God?

_____

_____

_____

_____

_____

_____

_____

_____

_____

_____

_____

_____

_____

_____

_____

_____

_____

_____

_____

_____

CONVERSATION 13

Savor the Moments

"Dear Brothers and Sisters when trouble of any kind come your way, consider it an opportunity for great joy." James 1:2 NLT

Have you ever logged unto Facebook and as soon as you opened the app. it immediately said, "We care about you and the memories you share here. We thought you'd like to look back on this post from years ago." Instantly, you begin to dwell on the status or picture that you posted from years ago. Have you ever read the status and it made you sit back and smile? Or did reading the status bring back a painful memory? Did you look at the picture and laugh because you could remember exactly what was going on in your life at that time? Or did you see the pain in your eyes or could you recognize your counterfeit smile?

One day while on my way to work, I read a message on the side of a bus, "Along your journey find moments to savor." I asked myself, what does it mean to savor the moment? It means to appreciate fully, enjoy or relish; to delight in. I love a good inspiration especially when I can see God in it. As I meditated on that message, it hit me that "your journey" is your life on this earth. Every millisecond that you breathe life, every decision that you make, and every action that you take all contribute to your journey. However, then I had a more profound understanding, that in life there are two journeys that you will experience.

The first one is a natural journey. On the natural or physical journey, you will experience ups and downs, mountains and valleys, twists and turns, joy and pain and everything in between. The tests, trials, and tribulations that you experience were meant to break you of your old self and build you into the person God has ordained you to be. Beware, on your natural journey. You may not understand why certain things are happening to you. These tough moments were orchestrated to strengthen you, change you, but most importantly draw you closer to God. As you draw closer to God, a shift begins to happen. Your thoughts start to change, your spiritual ears are fine-tuned, and your spiritual eyes are sharpened. You are now in a place where you can see your natural journey from God's perspective. Now you are ready to transition from your natural journey to the second journey. The second journey is the spiritual journey. You have learned that the good, the bad, and the ugly situations that you experienced were only intended to bless you. God tells us in Roman 8:28 NLT "and we know that God causes everything to work together for the good of those who love God and are called according to his purpose for them." During your spiritual journey, things are revealed to you, and you gain an understanding of why you went through everything that you experienced.

Maybe you experienced a year of unemployment or months of interviewing for jobs and still have not received a job offer. You cannot understand why God would open doors of opportunity for you and not bless you with employment. You then have a moment with God, and He reveals that He is preparing you. Maybe you have not interviewed in several years. During the interviewing process, He sharpened your skills. The previous interviews were just practice. He showed you through all the interviews what questions to ask. You have learned after research that an interview goes both ways. While the potential employer is interviewing you, you are also interviewing them to see if it's a good fit for you to work for their organization. At the RIGHT TIME, you are offered the job that you have been praying about. While God was preparing you for the position, He was working behind the scenes aligning the right people and company in your favor. You were offered the job because God had to prepare you to stand out from the rest of the candidates who interviewed for the same position. He aligned the right person to interview you because God qualified you for the position.

Have you experienced a failed relationship or are you holding on to a broken relationship that has expired according to God's plan for you? After the tears and heartache, you decide to surrender and to let go and let God. You've been praying to God to send you the man or woman that your heart desires, but this whole time God has been waiting for you to work on your relationship with Him. After all, that is the best relationship you will ever have. The bible tells us in Matthew 6:33, "put God first and everything else will fall into place." So, if you are not putting God first how do you expect to have a long-lasting relationship with a man or woman? During the intimate moments spent with God, you will realize that you may have neglected Him and have not taken the time to get to know Him honestly. The time that you spent with God will teach you that the other relationships did not work because God was not the foundation of that relationship.

You will learn how to forgive as God forgives. You will discover that TRUE love is pure, kind, and not jealous. You will learn to be obedient and allow God to strip you of your old ways of thinking to prepare you for the partner God has designed for you. At the RIGHT time when you are mentally, emotionally and spiritually ready, God will send you the man or woman that He has created for you. You will know that this time it's a godly relationship because God will send you who you need instead of who you want. When I think about all that I have experienced, I have learned to see GOD in EVERY situation. I have no choice but to savor the moments. I have come so far and still have a long way to go. Every time I share a testimony, I am savoring these moments because there was a time in my life that I knew of God but I did not know Him personally.

Do YOU know Him? We can all count our blessings, but are you finding moments to savor along your journey? When you genuinely KNOW Him, finding moments to savor along your journey will be nothing short of delightful. Your tests, trials, and tribulations are all moments to savor. When you come out on the side of victory, when God answers your prayers, reflect and say, "THANK YOU, LORD, for the lessons and blessings along my journey are moments that I savor."

Heart to Heart

Are you viewing your situation with your natural eye or from
a spiritual perspective?
Can you identify a moment that you savor?
Are you thankful for your life's journey including
the tough times?

_____

_____

_____

_____

_____

_____

_____

_____

_____

_____

_____

_____

_____

_____

_____

_____

_____

_____

_____

_____

CONVERSATION 14

Forgiveness

"For if you forgive others their sins, your heavenly Father will also forgive you. But if you do not forgive others, your Father will not forgive you your sins." Matthew 6:14-15 NLT

Disappointed. Betrayed. Hurt. Ashamed. Embarrassed. Lied to? Broken Hearted. Untrustworthy. We've all experienced these feelings before at some point in our lives. Someone we love has caused us to feel this way. Maybe a friend, close family member, or your spouse has done something to hurt you. Someone close to you did the unthinkable. What they did to you was unexpected. Their actions were unbelievable. The pain that they caused has left you with a broken heart, confused, resentful or in denial. You may have said to yourself, "How could this person that I love and care for do this to me?" In a split second your relationship with this person has changed for the worst.

Maybe your parent abandoned you as a child, and now as an adult, they want to have a relationship with you. Or maybe your spouse was unfaithful, or they lied to you. Or maybe a close friend does not support you like they do their other friends or maybe they have betrayed you. Whoever it is, and whatever they did, they hurt you in such a way that you feel that you cannot forgive them. We are all humans, and we all make mistakes. I'm sure in your life's journey that you have caused someone pain, hurt someone's feelings, or betrayed their trust. God instructs us to forgive each other throughout the Bible.

We sin daily causing God the same pain, hurt, and

agony that others cause us. When seeking God, do you expect Him to forgive you for everything you've done? Do you ask Him for forgiveness every time you fall short of His glory by doing things that are not pleasing to Him? Of course, we want God to forgive us because He is a forgiving God. I've heard people say "But I'm not God" in response to forgiving others. I reply no, you are not God, but God made us in His image. We are His sons and daughters, and He wants us to forgive others just like He forgives us. Life isn't easy, and we all have our share of flaws. This is not the first time, and this will not be the last time that someone along your life's path will hurt you. Remember that Jesus said in Matthew 18:22 NLT " Not seven times, I tell you, but seventy-seven times," is the number of times we are to forgive one another. It's a process, and you have to keep practicing forgiveness every day. Jesus died on the cross for our sins, and while on the cross He said, "Father forgive them, for they do not know what they are doing."

The next time that someone hurts you, think about all the times you have fallen short, done or said things that were not pleasing to God. Think about how He forgave you and showered you with grace and mercy instead of punishing you. TRUST ME, forgiveness is one of the hardest things to do in life, and it does not happen overnight. You have to take steps to be open to forgiving. Most importantly forgive yourself so that you can live a life that's free from holding on to anger and grudges. Forgive so that you can move forward and live a life that is pleasing to God. Ask God to give you strength to let go of past disappointments and to bless you with a clean and pure heart so that you can make room for forgiveness to live inside of you.

Heart to Heart

Is it difficult for you to forgive?
Why are you still holding on to pain?
Is the pain benefiting you?
In what ways can you begin to forgive those that have
hurt you?

_____

_____

_____

_____

_____

_____

_____

_____

_____

_____

_____

_____

_____

_____

_____

_____

_____

_____

_____

CONVERSATION 15

Purpose For The Pain

"For I consider that our present sufferings cannot even be compared to the glory that will be revealed to us." Romans 8:18 NLT

Pain is physical suffering or discomfort caused by illness or injury. Pain is something that no one wants to experience, but no one is exempt from feeling pain. If you wish to believe it or not, there is a purpose for the pain. Pain allows you to appreciate the sunny days. Pain forces you to grow. Pain reveals things about you that you have not been willing to acknowledge. Pain draws you nearer to God. Pain will force you to your knees and cry out to God. God will inflict pain upon you so that He can reveal Himself to you. The purpose of suffering is for God to receive all the glory when you overcome the pain. Anytime pain is inflicted upon you; you must realize that it is taking you to your next level. The next level that God has called you on is in your spiritual relationship with Him.

Jesus was sent into this world to experience life in human form. Do you think that God would exempt us from feeling the same pain that Jesus felt? While on the cross Jesus asked God in Luke 22:42 NLT "Father, if you are willing, please take this cup of suffering away from me. Yet I want your will to be done, not mine." Guess what? It was not God's will to remove the suffering from him. God responded in 2 Corinthians 12:9 NLT "My grace is all you need. My power works best in weakness." God had a purpose for Jesus' pain. The purpose was for Jesus to take on our sins so that we can have eternal life and a direct relationship with God. The present suffering that you are experiencing will not last forever.

When you grow through the pain, you will have no choice but to give God all the glory, honor, and praise. Your pain could help someone who is or is getting ready to experience what you are going through or have previously endured. Your pain will show you how strong you truly are. Your pain will also show you that you are experiencing every aspect of life. After the dark clouds and when the storm has passed, the pain will be a distant memory to prove that you are victorious and an overcomer.

My pastor always says, "It may not feel good while it's working, but its working for your good." After the pain, you will find out the purpose. Sometimes while you are experiencing pain, God will send someone along your path for you to speak to and encourage you that it will get better. Even through your pain, God will use you as a vessel, and it will bring healing to you as you help others.

Heart to Heart

Do you believe that there is a purpose for pain?
Are you able to recognize the good in the pain?
Or are you consumed with why did things happen?
Have you experienced pain before and something good
came out of it?

_____

_____

_____

_____

_____

_____

_____

_____

_____

_____

_____

_____

_____

_____

_____

_____

_____

_____

_____

_____

CONVERSATION 16

Above All

"Now to him who is able to do exceedingly abundantly above all that we ask or think, according to the power that works in us."
Ephesians 3:20 NKJV

Do you understand how big, mighty, and powerful God is? Often we tend to put limitations on God so that our natural minds can comprehend. God is so much greater than that. He wants us to come to Him with bold prayers, big faith, and unlimited imagination. God wants to show up in your life to prove that He is God and everything is possible with Him. We may start off with simple prayers and get excited when God answers them, but there is a power that is at work within us. This is the same power that raised Jesus Christ from the dead after three days. Now that's powerful and beyond anything that humans can comprehend. God wants us to tap into that power to pray bold prayers because He can do ABOVE ALL we could ever imagine.

God may have placed a desire in your heart that you have been praying for but have yet to see it come to pass. You begin to get anxious, fear starts to creep into your spirit (God did not give us a spirit of fear), and now you are at the point where you want to give up and quit. It is written in James 5:16 NLT "The effectual fervent prayer of the righteous availeth much." In other words, the power that is inside of you, use it with all your might and persistently pray and believe that it will come to pass. God desires that we have and live a life full of abundance. He wants to answer those prayers and add more to it. God's way is not our way, and His thoughts are more significant than ours. Do not confine God to a box where your natural eye cannot see past the present waiting period. Tap into the power that's at work within you and believe and have faith that God will do above all that you are praying for. Pray the impossible, expect the unexpected, and dream the unimaginable because we serve an above all God.

Heart to Heart

Do you understand how powerful God is?
Are you limiting God's power to what you're able to understand?
Do you believe that God can do exceedingly and abundantly above all that you can imagine?

_____

_____

_____

_____

_____

_____

_____

_____

_____

_____

_____

_____

_____

_____

_____

_____

_____

_____

_____

_____

CONVERSATION 17

Be Still

"Be still and know that I am God." Psalms 46:10 NLT

There's a storm raging inside of you. There's a storm roaring on the outside of you. Your mind is racing, and your spirit is uneasy. You are drowning in anxiety and fear. What do you do? Try to handle the situation on your own by taking matters into your own hands? No! Be Still! You may ask, "how can I be still when it feels like everything is falling apart?" I know that it's easier said than done. I understand that this a challenge for many us. This has been a personal struggle of mine as well. God is and will forever be the answer to helping us to be still. In the Bible, it instructs us numerous times to be still, because God will fight our battles. This battle is not ours to fight; it's the Lords. When you're not in control of the situation, how do quiet your concerns?

For starters, take a deep breath. Inhale peace and exhale panic. Seek God. He has given us power and authority to speak life over ourselves. Speak over yourself and rebuke thoughts and feelings that are not aligned with the will of God. Rebuke the chains that are keeping you captive and the voices from your mind that are not of God. Try to quiet your thoughts. Do you enjoy music? Listen to songs that soothe your soul. I love to hear *Total Praise* by Anita Wilson, or *I told the Storm* by Greg O'Quin 'N Joyful Noyze. Or consider finding a scripture to meditate on day and night. I love Psalms 46:10 Be still and know that I am God. I believe that it's so easy to remember and so powerful to speak out loud. Confess to God that you need Him. Ask Him to help you to keep your mind, heart, and spirit still. Find a song to listen to that will keep your spirit calm.

Maintain an attitude of gratitude. The only way to wholeheartedly trust God and His process is to surrender all to Him. Surrendering to God's will and releasing your own will help the process of fortifying your stillness. Until you have mastered being still, praise God and tell Him how mighty, majestic, amazing, and wonderful He is. Remind yourself of the good things that He has done for you in the past. Reflecting on God's goodness is a great way to get into a peaceful state.

There are many ways to exercise stillness; these are just some examples for you to ponder as you work towards being still. While you are working on being still, God is working on your behalf. Work on having a spirit of expectancy, because after all if you know God for yourself then you know there's no need to worry. Every day spend more and more time with God and His word. If today you spent five minutes with him, increase it tomorrow by another five minutes. This will help you to focus more on God than on your storm. You will eventually start to feel a change and see a difference in your circumstances.

Most importantly, let God be God. He does not need our help to fix the situation. He's already gone ahead and worked everything out. He's sent his angels ahead of you to make your crooked path straight. All God asks is for you to relax, be still, and watch him work.

Heart to Heart

Are you in a place where you feel as though everything
is falling apart?
Do you try to control the situation or are you still
and giving it to God?
What are some ways that you can practice to become still?

_____

_____

_____

_____

_____

_____

_____

_____

_____

_____

_____

_____

_____

_____

_____

_____

_____

_____

_____

_____

CONVERSATION 18

Be Comfortable with Being Uncomfortable

"He cuts off every branch of mine that does not produce fruit, and he
prunes the branches that do bear fruit so they will produce even more."
John 15:2 NLT

Pruning is the process of trimming a tree, shrub, or bush by cutting away dead or overgrown branches or stems, mainly to increase fruitfulness and growth. Also, it reduces the extent of something by removing unwanted parts. Talk about being uncomfortable. As Christians, God is our true vine, and we are the branches that are connected to Him. There are habits, thoughts, actions, and ways that are not pleasing to God that He wants to prune us from. He wants to prune us of these things that are not of Him so that we can grow and become the person He has called us to be. The pruning period usually occurs during a trial, tribulation, or challenge.

No one likes to be uncomfortable, but discomfort is the only way that God can reach us. When you feel the discomfort, the pain, the sadness, the disappointment, know that the pruning process has begun. The pruning process was never intended to be comfortable. When you are uncomfortable in your situation, that's an indication that growth is on the way. Do not fight it allow God to get rid of the "dead things" that are not helping you to grow and become a better version of yourself. Feel all the feelings that are exiting your body. Get comfortable with allowing God to prune you. Once you get comfortable with being uncomfortable, the pruning process can run its course the way God intended it to.

Many people choose to run away from anything that causes discomfort. It is easier to remain comfortable because of fear of experiencing pain or moving into unfamiliar space of something new, but God has not called us to remain comfortable. To grow and to get to the next level, God has to step in and make us uncomfortable; I encourage you to step out of your comfort zone and embrace the discomfort. The place of discomfort will mold and shape you. God is using discomfort to work in you, through you, and for you. God has greater things in store for you if you learn how to be comfortable with being uncomfortable. The minute you stop growing because you're uncomfortable, scared of change or fear of the unknown is when you settle for less than. You're not meant to stay the same. You are intended to grow and become who God ordained you to be.

Heart to Heart

Do you run away when life gets uncomfortable?
Or do you face the discomfort?
Are you willing to be uncomfortable to change and grow into
a better person?

_____

_____

_____

_____

_____

_____

_____

_____

_____

_____

_____

_____

_____

_____

_____

_____

_____

_____

_____

_____

_____

CONVERSATION 19

It Only Gets Better

"Look straight ahead and fix your eyes on what lies before you."
Proverbs 4:25 NLT

If you lived long enough, then you've experienced some trial, test, or tribulation. In that same instance, you have also experienced love, joy, peace, happiness and countless blessings. Imagine being on the mountaintop and your life seems to be going exactly the way you planned it. God is answering all your prayers, and this is your season of abundance. You're smiling, rejoicing in the Lord, and at peace. You cannot think of life getting any better, after all; things are aligning up in your favor. Then out of nowhere, your favor comes to a screeching halt! Uh oh, what just happened? You were knocked off the mountaintop, and you have landed in the valley.

Discombobulated, you try to figure out exactly how did you end up in the valley. You ask God, "I thought this was my season of blessings? Did I do something wrong? ...Hello, God can you hear me?" Ecclesiastes 3:1 NLT states, For everything, there is a season, a time for every activity under heaven." Often in life, we get knocked off the mountaintop and land in the valley because God is getting ready to do something new in our lives. The only way to get to that new place is to go through the valley. Nothing about being in the valley is pretty. Let's be clear it is ugly but, when you come out what a beautiful sight it will be.

You may feel like Job, where everything God has blessed you with has been taken away from you. The job, the relationship, the home, or even the car that He provided you with, you felt like it was stripped away from you. What we sometimes fail to realize is that when God takes something from us, He will always replace it with something better than we could ever imagine. So, when you are in the valley, keep your eyes focused on what is in front of you. The best days of your life are ahead of you. If you thought the good days were on your last mountaintop, you haven't seen anything yet. The new mountaintop will be higher than the one in the previous season. If He has done it before, He will do it again. Where God is taking you is in front of you so keep your eyes focused on Him. The past is behind you. Have you ever thought about why God placed your eyes on your face? My theory is to remind us that our eyes are in front of us to look forward and not behind.

Heart to Heart

Do you think that you have already experienced the
best days of your life?
Do you believe that God has better things instore for you?
Are you expecting new blessings to come your way?

_____

_____

_____

_____

_____

_____

_____

_____

_____

_____

_____

_____

_____

_____

_____

_____

_____

_____

_____

_____

CONVERSATION 20

Speak It Into Existence!

"Now faith is the substance of things hoped for, the evidence of."
Hebrews 11:1 NLT

Have you ever imagined something that seemed so real that you could practically see it in front you? Or maybe your imagination created the fibers of that thing in such a way that you could have stretched your hand right out and touched it? Although that thing that you so desperately yearn for hasn't manifested in the natural form, in your mind, it is already real. This is the kind of faith you need to manifest your deepest desires. You will have to visualize it before you can see it. Your imagination is a God-given tool that can literally build out your desires through faith.

Every year since my 27th birthday I've celebrated my birthday on vacation with my girls. For my 30th birthday, my friends and I went to St. Martin, and we HAD A BLAST! While on vacation, something inside of me felt like I wanted a change. I had outgrown my newly found tradition. I realized that for my 31st birthday I wanted to do something different. I told my friends, "I love y'all, but next year I'm going on a baecation with my boo!" Translated, a baecation is a vacation with your "bae"/significant other. I bet you're wondering well why didn't I go away with my boo for my 30th birthday? Well, I did not have a boo at that stage in my life. At 30 years old, I had never been on a "baecation," and it was something that I knew I wanted to experience in my thirties. On October 18, 2014, my focus shifted. I yearned for companionship and in November 2014, I started telling my friends about "my boo." I did not know what "my boo" looked like, where he was from, nor did I know when he would enter into my life. However, what I did know was that my boo would be coming soon.

I knew in my heart that he was on his way. I went to the extent of creating a vision board with images of a man, a couple, love, and vacations to represent my forthcoming romance. This visual kept me encouraged. I placed the vision board on my altar right next to my Bible to keep me encouraged. During that time I was not in a relationship, and I decided to let go and let God change the state of my sad love life. I started to pray to God and thank Him in advance for the man that He had in store for me. Over the next few months, I continued to speak him into existence. My faith reassured me that my mate was coming soon. In April 2015, my boo finally showed up, and he was more than I could have imagined.

The funny thing about my life is that I had actually met him in May 2014, but it was a brief encounter. We met at my friend's event on Cinco de Mayo. Now fast-forward to almost a year later, we met again at a brunch that he and another mutual friend coordinated. I arrived at the brunch late and ended up sitting next to him. I kept saying to him and a mutual friend that we met before, but I could not figure out where. She said, "you probably met him at one of my birthday functions," but I knew that was not it. It was not until after an in-depth conversation with him that I believed the Holy Spirit led me to ask him where he worked. He told me where he worked and it finally clicked! I pulled out my phone and asked him if this was his number? At that moment we laughed, and we realized that we met at the Cinco de Mayo event in 2014 almost a year to the date prior. After the brunch, we started dating, and he became my boo. We have so many things in common, including our birthdays. It turned out that his birthday is in October too, only six days before mine. Guess what? The baecation MANIFESTED! We went on a cruise to the

REAL TALK

Bahamas! Exactly a year after my 30th birthday, my heart desire manifested. I wanted to share and to encourage you that there is power in your words.

When God created the earth, he said "Let there be light," and there was light Genesis 1:3. Know that God has given you power and authority to speak over your life. God will provide you with the desires of your heart if you trust in Him, have faith, and believe. Whatever it is that you are hoping for, act as if you already have it. Thank God in advance for blessing you with your heart desires.

Heart to Heart

What do you believe in your mind that you
cannot see with your physical eyes yet?
Is your faith assuring you that what you are speaking into
existence is on the way?
What tools do you use to remind you of your heart's desire?

_____

_____

_____

_____

_____

_____

_____

_____

_____

_____

_____

_____

_____

_____

_____

_____

_____

_____

_____

CONVERSATION 21

Do You Want A Good Thing Or A God Thing?

"All these blessings will come to you in abundance if you obey the Lord your God." Deuteronomy 28:2 NLT

When you hear, "A good thing," you may think it's a good thing that's meant to last right? After all, you prayed about it, and God has answered your prayers. What if the good thing was only seasonal? It's like that old saying, "all good things come to an end." What happens when your good thing's season expires? Do you hold on and try to keep a tight grasp on it? Alternatively, do you let go and reach for the God thing? Good things aren't meant to last forever. Whatever your good thing may be, ask yourself is God telling you to let it go and let him work a God thing for you? I believe that things in life are here for a reason, season, and a lifetime. Wouldn't you rather have a "thing" that is here for a lifetime, since lifetime placements are God things? God wants to send you things that add value to your life to maximize your ultimate abundance. It is quite difficult to let go of things that God may have given you that were only meant for a season, especially if it was "your" heart desires. You can get over those temporary things and move forward in your life to obtain your lifetime blessings. Through the process remember that it will be worth it and that you deserve God's blessing that will last a lifetime.

Have you considered that maybe the season has ended because God is taking you to a new level in Him? He sure is. He's molding and shaping you to be more like

Him; therefore, the good thing that you once wanted no longer serves its purpose for where God is taking you. He is taking you to a new level and to a higher dimension in your faith, hope, prayer life, and trust in Him. The "good thing" that He gave you was based on your level of faith during that season. However, it is time to grow and take your obedience to the next level.

This new level requires you to pray bigger prayers, expect bigger blessings, and dream bigger dreams. The only way to get to that level is to surrender your heart entirely to God. Surrender your will and your wants. Surrender the good thing so that you can get the God thing. I know you're probably thinking, "I have to surrender?" That's been a challenge for me as well. It's not always easy to surrender all to God or to even obey God.

What are your reservations? Have you thought, "what if I follow God and He tells me something I don't want to hear or what if He doesn't answer my prayer? What if He's telling me to obey and let go of that good thing?" Now is the time to change your thinking to, "God wants me to let go because He has something better for me." I faced the same challenges of surrendering my whole heart to God in fear of the "ifs." By surrendering all to God and obeying Him, He will give you new desires for your heart that will match the faith that you need to go to the next level. To receive all the blessings and abundance, obey God and surrender to Him so that you can receive the God things He is preparing you for. It's working out for your good. What God wants to bless you with is far better than a good thing. The God thing is going to last, and most importantly God will be glorified through it.

Heart to Heart

Do you want a good thing or a God thing?
What are you holding onto that is keeping you from letting go
of the good thing?
Are you ready to surrender to receive the God thing?

_____

_____

_____

_____

_____

_____

_____

_____

_____

_____

_____

_____

_____

_____

_____

_____

_____

_____

_____

_____

CONVERSATION 22

Great Things Are Birthed Through Pain

"This brings you great joy, although you may have to suffer for a short time in various trials." 1 Peter 1:6 NET

Who on this earth wants to suffer or experience pain, anguish, and hurt? No one wants to suffer. If Jesus suffered, we are not exempt from suffering, trials, and tribulations. It's only through pain that we will then experience joy. It's only through pain that great things are birthed. Childbirth is the perfect example. For nine months women carry a baby. Their bodies are changing and experiencing discomfort and pain. When the contractions occur, and as it gets closer to delivery time the pain is intensified. I do not have children, and I can only imagine the amount of pain that a woman must endure during the birthing process, After hours of labor, the greatest gift in life has been birthed. After admiring your beautiful blessing, the pain becomes a distant memory. The pain that some women have said they endured for short or extensive times does not compare to the blessing of a lifetime from the delivery. It is while you're experiencing significant pain that great things are about to be birthed into your life.

Maybe during this short time of pain, you were given the idea to write a book that you have been thinking about. The pain of a particular situation provided you with material to write about. Your book will be birthed after your pain. Or the pain that you are feeling birthed in you the idea to become an entrepreneur and form your own organization. It's not until after the pain has stopped that the great thing is birthed. The joy you will experience after the pain will not compare to the temporary pain and suffering that you may face. God allows conflict because He has a greater purpose that is going to birth a great thing. How would you know what a great thing is if you never experienced pain and or a bad thing? God could be using pain to birth in you a new thing by shedding the old layers. He's making you a new person, and the only way to become new is to go through discomfort. Birth signifies new beginnings. Think about a time when you received a new car, home, or job. Do you remember the bliss that you felt? That's the joy that God wants us to experience, but only after we have suffered for a little while. No matter what the great thing that is being birthed in you, remember to receive the great thing you must go through the pain. No pain, no Godly gain.

Heart to Heart

Do you believe that great things are birthed through pain?
Have you currently experienced pain and an idea was
birthed in you as a result?
What are some ways that you can use your pain
to execute the idea that was birthed in you?

_____

_____

_____

_____

_____

_____

_____

_____

_____

_____

_____

_____

_____

_____

_____

_____

_____

_____

_____

_____

CONVERSATION 23

God is in Your Neighborhood

"Yet I am confident I will see the Lord's goodness while I am here in the land of the living." Psalm 27:13 NLT

Have you and the people in your life ever experienced a season of trials at the same time? During the trial or dry season, you all are praying for each other and yourselves. Periodically you check in on each other to send each other encouraging words of peace and hope. Next thing you know, things are starting to turn around in their situation. You see that God has brought them out of their dry season and placed them into their promised land. It's natural to think, "What about me? God, I must be next, right?" You're happy to see God's hand at work in their life. You know that it is only a matter of time before your situation turns around in your favor. The fact that God is blessing those close to you means that He is in your neighborhood and your blessings are on the way.

It can become discouraging to witness God answer the prayers of others and not yours. Do not focus too much on your friend or family member's blessings that you take your eyes off the Lord. God blessing them should give you a confident hope that you are seeing the goodness of the Lord in the land of the living. Maybe God blessed them first because their home is at the top of the block in the neighborhood and God has not made His way to your part of the street. God is doing a new thing for you too, but maybe He has to take more time to prepare you to receive what you have been praying for. Your prayers could be more detailed, and God is ensuring that everything about your blessing is just right.

What do you do while you wait for God to reach your doorstep? You stir up the mustard seed of faith that is planted within you. You get excited about what God is about to do. You praise Him in advance. You thank Him in advance for the blessing that's about to show up in your life. Get your confidence ready because you know that you serve a God that is a good God. Take an inventory of your memory bank to reflect on the times He has blessed you in the past. Have assurance that what God did for them, He can also do for you. Do not fret, rejoice in the Lord, and get ready to receive your blessing. When you least expect it, after God has blessed others in your neighborhood, He will knock on your door. Will you be home to answer the door for Him?

Heart to Heart

Do you ask God, "what about me?"
Is your focus on God or is it on everyone's blessings?
What blessing are you waiting for?
Do you believe that you are next in line to receive
your blessing?

_____

_____

_____

_____

_____

_____

_____

_____

_____

_____

_____

_____

_____

_____

_____

_____

_____

_____

_____

_____

CONVERSATION 24

Are you Prepared for What You're Praying For?

"The effective, fervent prayer of a righteous man avails much."
James 5:16 NKJV
"Pray without ceasing." 1 Thessalonians 5:17 NKJV

Are you a person who is impatient? Does your patience run thin while waiting in line to pay for items at the grocery store? Or how about when you are driving behind a car that's driving below the speed limit? I think that we have all experienced our patience deplete to zero. Have you prayed to God and asked Him to give you patience? The minute you release that prayer you feel the rain clouds over your head. You may think, "God all I wanted was patience, why did you send a storm?" Have you decided that you want to take your relationship with God to the next level? All of a sudden you notice that God takes away the thing that you have wanted for so long. For example, if you've been praying for a promotion at work and you were denied, or you want to take the next steps with your significant other and a situation arises within the relationship, or if you have prayed for a financial breakthrough and your circumstances change where you are behind in all your bills.

God will send tests your way that are contrary to what you have been praying about. Are you prepared for the test or do you only want to reap the benefits of the answered prayer? Often, preparation comes before the answered prayers. God wants to know if you will trust Him as He prepares you to receive your answered prayers.

Just like in school when you take a test, you have to prepare for the test so that you can earn a passing grade. How do you prepare for the test? By studying feverishly and memorizing the information until you know it by heart. It is not easy but being prepared is the only way that you will pass the test. You can walk into the classroom with confidence because you know that you have studied and that you are ready to be tested. The same goes for preparing for what you're praying for. As God sends tests your way, continue to develop yourself by praying fervently and trusting that God will see you through. Through trials continue to pray because they are only temporary.

You cannot have a test without a testimony. Prayer is the way through the test. You must endure trials that will test your faith and character to become the person that is ready to receive the answered prayer. Continue to pray because it's all about growth and becoming more like Christ. God wants you to put your trust in Him and obey Him. Storms will come that will test your patience and faith in God. Tests prepare you for the next level. The next time you ask for patience or ask to go to the next level in God, prepare yourself for the tests that will come before the answered prayer.

Heart to Heart

Are you prepared for what you have been praying for?
Can you identify a test that God has sent you as He prepares you for your blessing?
What do you think the lesson is that you need to learn from the test?

_____

_____

_____

_____

_____

_____

_____

_____

_____

_____

_____

_____

_____

_____

_____

_____

_____

_____

_____

_____

CONVERSATION 25

The Waiting Room

"Wait patiently for the Lord. Be brave and courageous. Yes, wait patiently for the Lord." Psalms 27:14 NLT

Waiting? Who likes to wait? Waiting for test results from your Doctor, waiting in traffic, or waiting for a vacation, can cause you to become impatient. None of those scenarios test your patience like the waiting you endure while you're in the "waiting room of your life." Have you been in the waiting room believing God to manifest the promises over your life, wondering how much longer do I have to stay here? The waiting room is the place that you find yourself in after you have experienced trials and tribulations. After God has moved you beyond those trials, you graduate to a place where you are healed and find peace knowing that what you have just experienced was working for your good. As you transition from your preparation season of sowing seeds to the harvest season of reaping the benefits, there's always a season of waiting. This in-between stage is where you should be getting excited about the blessings that are coming your way. Start thanking God in advance for what He already has done.

There will be times when you feel impatient and discouraged witnessing others in their harvest season receiving the blessings that God has for them. The moment you begin to ask "God, when is it my turn?" Or "Where are my blessings?" Shift your focus and ask God for His perfect peace that surpasses all understanding. Know that what He has planned for you is better than anything you could have ever imagined. The Bible teaches us to wait patiently for God. Waiting essentially means to be expectant. While we wait, we should praise God. We should tell God how great and mighty He is. How wonderful His works are and that they are worth the wait.

Remember the times in your life that God provided immense blessings over your life. God wants to perform wonderful works in the lives of his children, but some blessings take longer than others for Him to prepare you for. While you're waiting on God, take your faith, praise, and worship to the next level. While you're in the waiting room and witnessing other people's numbers in line get called for their blessing, know that you are next in line. Take your mind off the fact that you're waiting and thank God that your number will be called next. It was written, "That a day is like a thousand years to the Lord, and a thousand years is like a day (2 Peter 3:8)." Wait patiently for the Lord, because what He's preparing for you is going to be worth the wait.

Heart to Heart

Are you currently in the "waiting room" waiting for God to answer your prayers?

How do you react when God sends someone their blessing while you are in the waiting room together?

What are you doing while you are waiting?

_____

_____

_____

_____

_____

_____

_____

_____

_____

_____

_____

_____

_____

_____

_____

_____

_____

_____

_____

CONVERSATION 26

Take Back Your Power

"A final word: Be strong in the Lord and in his mighty power. Put on all of God's armor so that you will be able to stand firm against all strategies of the devil."
Ephesians 6:10-11 NLT

The enemy is out to attack your mind, body, and spirit. He will use every weapon in his arsenal to take you down. His attacks are personal because he knows that God has great things in store for you. Have you ever woke up and asked God to show you a sign that what you are praying for is in His will for your life? He answers you by showing you a sign that you were looking for and your hope and joy is restored. All of a sudden, as you are going about your day, you feel your joy leave your spirit. You're in a state of confusion wondering what just happened. Maybe a friend of yours reached out to you to chat and brings up a topic that you have been praying about, and you feel your spirit transition to an unsettled state. The joy and hope you felt earlier in the day has left entirely. Your spirit becomes anxious, and you know that it's not from God. What do you do at that moment? Let the enemy steal your joy and take you out? Do you put on the full armor of God and take your power back?

God has given us power and authority over the enemy. He did not create us to worry or to fear. He definitely did not create us to be defeated because we are more than conquerors. The minute you feel your spirit shift from peace to doubt, worry, or defeat that's when you pull out your weapons against the enemy. Your weapons are scriptures and words that affirm victory. Say to yourself , "I have on the full armor of God. In the name of Jesus no weapon formed against shall prosper. I am more than a conqueror, and If God is for me, who can be against me?" Repeat this to yourself over and over again. If you are at home or in your car, shout these verses out loud. Or maybe you are at work or in a public place, whisper these phrases to yourself as you sit at your desk, or while walking to your office. Do not let the enemy use tactics and or strategies to make you doubt what you heard God say and what He has shown you. Tell the enemy, "In the name of Jesus you must flee." You are a child of God who has power. The full armor of God and your spiritual weapons are what you will need to defeat the enemy and take your power back.

Heart to Heart

Has the enemy been attacking your mind, heart,
and or spirit?
Are you aware of the power that dwells within you?
What tactics are you using to take your power back?

_____

_____

_____

_____

_____

_____

_____

_____

_____

_____

_____

_____

_____

_____

_____

_____

_____

_____

_____

CONVERSATION 27

Provision Follows The Vision

"Abraham named the place Yah-weh Yireh (which means "the Lord will provide"). To this day, people still use that name as a proverb. "On the mountain of the Lord, it will be provided." Genesis 22:14 NLT

Provision is the act of providing or supplying for use or an amount or thing supplied or provided. Did you know that Jehovah- Jireh means God will provide? Has God given you a heart's desire and you wonder to yourself how am I going to make this happen? Or have you ever wondered, I don't know if this is even possible? Have you ever thought to yourself that if God has given you a vision, He will provide everything you need to be successful? Do you have a vision of starting your own business and don't know how it is going to work out? God will open doors for you that will align you with the right people to come into your life to help you become successful. Maybe God has given you the vision to go back to school. You may think to yourself, "how am going to work full-time and go to school?" God will provide you with opportunities to find programs that offer online, evening and weekend class options so that you can successfully do both.

Perhaps you want a new car but feel as though you can't afford it. You decide to go to the dealership to test drive the car anyway, and God aligned you with a salesman who was able to help you drive off the lot with a new car the same day without putting any money down. Maybe you have been searching for the job of your dreams, and a friend of yours is a recruiter at a company that is the perfect fit for you. You end up getting the job because God aligned your friend to work for the company first so that they were able to help you get the job you've been dreaming of.

No matter what the vision is that God has planted in your heart, He will always provide and make sure that it comes to pass. Often God uses people, circumstances, and divine connections to provide you with everything you need to make your vision manifest. The next time God gives you a vision thank Him in advance for providing every single thing that you need to implement your vision.

Heart to Heart

What vision has God given you?
Are you trying to figure out how it is going to work out?
Do you know that God will supply all your needs?

_____

_____

_____

_____

_____

_____

_____

_____

_____

_____

_____

_____

_____

_____

_____

_____

_____

_____

_____

_____

_____

_____

CONVERSATION 28

Are You A Man/Woman of God? Or Do You Believe in God?

"God created humankind in his image, in the image of God he created them, male and female he created them." Genesis 1: 27 NET

God created humankind, which means that we are His children. Just because you are a child of God, does not mean that we are men and women of God. It could mean that we believe in God because He is a higher being. A believer in God knows things about Him, but that does not mean that they have a relationship with God. They know that God is good. They may also know that God blesses people and answers prayers. However, do they know Him?

Men and women of God have a relationship with God where they put Him first. They know and understand that when you put God first, everything will fall into place. Men and women of God seek to hear His voice and get to know Him on every level. They intentionally set aside time to spend in His word to learn the characteristics of God, but also so that they can apply Gods word to their life. Prayer is the way they know how to communicate with God. Believers understand that prayer is the only way that their situation will change, or that God's will is for their prayer to change them through their situation. No matter what the situation looks like they continue to trust God.

Characteristics of men and women of God are God-fearing, longing to serve God and to do His will. They seek God daily, repent their sins and ask for forgiveness while forgiving those who have done them wrong. Their hearts yearn, love, pursue and thirst for Him. They praise and worship God while giving God all the glory for all that He's done, doing, and getting ready to do. They have a heart desire to magnify the Lord because they know that without God they are nothing. They walk confidently yet humbled because they know that God walks with them daily. They know how to encourage themselves as well as those around them. Most importantly, men and women of God know that they are not perfect but strive to live righteously and to be more like Christ. They surrender their will to God because they recognize that His will is better than any decision that they could make.

I know it may seem hard to be a man or woman of God, but allowing God and the Holy Spirit to lead, guide, and direct your path is how you go from being a believer in God to becoming a man and woman of God. The straight and narrow path is less traveled because it is hard; however, the reward is far greater than the broad path. Do you want to remain a believer who knows of God? Or are you ready and willing to become a man or woman of God that knows God and has a personal relationship with Him?

Heart to Heart

Are you a man/woman of God?
Or do you believe in God?
In what ways do you want to mature spiritually?

_____

_____

_____

_____

_____

_____

_____

_____

_____

_____

_____

_____

_____

_____

_____

_____

_____

_____

CONVERSATION 29

A New You

"Don't copy the behavior and customs of this world, but let God transform you into a new person by changing the way you think." Romans 12:2 NLT

Are you tired of doing the same thing over and over again expecting different results? Are you burnt out and exhausted from trying to make things happen in your own strength? The person you are may be broken, and you may be living a life that God did not design for you. Have you had enough and want to be a new person? Maybe God isn't trying to improve your situation; He's trying to improve you in the situation. Are you interested in changing who you are, to become a new and improved version of yourself? The question you might ask yourself is how do I change? Where do I begin? The first step is acknowledging and accepting that you no longer want to be the current version of yourself.

Research suggests that it takes 21 days to form or break a habit, so what are the steps to becoming a new you? First, ask God to change your heart. Ask Him to create in you a clean and pure heart. Ask Him to remove all impurities from your heart. Ask God to fill your heart with love, joy, forgiveness, hope, faith, wisdom, knowledge, understanding, courage, and confidence. Ask God for His perfect peace that surpasses all understanding. Ask Him for positive thoughts. Ask God to transform your thoughts and to renew your mind. Ask God to fine-tune your spiritual ears so that you can hear him clearly. Ask God to remove the veil from your eyes so that He can reveal Himself to you ensuring that you feel His presence. Ask God to sharpen your spiritual eyes so that you can see things from God's perspective. Ask God to align your thoughts with His thoughts. Seek God and ask Him to renew in you a new spirit. Ask God to cut off branches that are not producing any fruit in your life. Ask God to purge and prune you of your old ways, thoughts, and habits that are not helping you to become the person God has ordained you to be.

The fundamental principle of changing into a new and improved version of yourself is to simply spend time in God's word. Challenge yourself to make time for God by reading His word for the next 21-days to learn about Him for yourself. Confess your sins and seek His forgiveness. The more you understand God's word, the more you will change and become like Him. Have an attitude of gratitude. Rejoice in His goodness. These are just some ways to start the process of becoming a new you. If you spend time with God for 21-days straight, you will form a habit, which will result in a new you. Get out of your way and allow God to work in you. You will become a new version of yourself, your best version yet!

Heart to Heart

Are you tired of doing the same thing and getting the
same results?
Do you want to become renewed?
What are you willing to change to become the best version
of yourself?

_____

_____

_____

_____

_____

_____

_____

_____

_____

_____

_____

_____

_____

_____

_____

_____

_____

_____

_____

_____

_____

CONVERSATION 30

God's Plan

"For I know the plans I have for you," says the Lord. "They are plans for good and not for disaster, to give you a future and a hope."
Jeremiah 29:11 NLT

If you would have asked me on January 1st, 2018 if I thought the plans that God had planned for me up until June 2018 were for my good, I'd tell you that it "felt" more like a disaster. The plans that I had for myself were not exactly what God had in store for me in the first six months of 2018. Proverbs 16:9 NLT states "We can make our plans, but the Lord determines our steps." I had an awakening this year that proved this scripture to be true. Three of the goals that I wrote down for 2018 were to take my relationship with God to the next level, write a book and publish one devotional on my favorite blog called *The Praying Woman*. My plans for taking my relationship with God to the next level included being more verbal in my praise and worship, trying to memorize more scriptures, seeking Him more, and allowing God to use me. Of course, when I wrote down the goals, I did not think about what they would entail.

God's plan to get me to my next level in Him was not an easy maneuver. I did not foresee that it was going to cost me some things, I would endure some things, and I would have to let go of some things. God's plan was for me to surrender my will and wants for His will and wants for Him to use me. I learned that to get to that next level in God He had to inflict pain, send oppositions my way, and cause me to suffer for a while. God needed to grow me, stretch me, purge me, and even isolate me at times. I was not aware that the confusion, disappointment, and moments of lack of faith that was orchestrated by God were meant for me to help people in a significant way. I would have no idea that there were people who were going to need me to encourage, inspire, and help them this year.

As I endured my trials and tribulations, I began to write. I revealed to a friend about my goal of publishing one devotional she told me "You need to create your own blog. God has too much inside of you for anything small like one devotional. You just wanted to write, but God wants you to do bigger things." She was right; God had given me more than enough content from my own experiences and people that He sent my way to write and publish just one devotional. It was at that moment that I realized what God's plan for me in 2018 was. He had to stop the plans I made for myself because He was in need of me to do something more significant. He gave me experiences to create my blog praytheimpossible.com and to not only finish writing this devotional book but to publish it as well. God's plan for my life produced *Real Talk; A Conversation From my Heart to Yours* and my blog to provide people with tools to find encouragement, inspiration, and help.

The suffering I experienced for a little while was never about me; He needed to use me to reach people outside of my close circle. I want to hearten and assure you that God's plans are always bigger than our plans. No matter what you are going through it is all according to God's plans. Even though it may "feel" like it's a disaster trust me, it gets better. It is actually working for your good and the greater good of God's Kingdom.

Heart to Heart

What are the plans that you made for yourself?
Are they aligned with God's plan for you?
Is God's plan changing you into the person He has
called you to become?

_____

_____

_____

_____

_____

_____

_____

_____

_____

_____

_____

_____

_____

_____

_____

_____

_____

_____

_____

REAL TALK: A CONVERSATION FROM MY HEART TO YOURS

The preceding conversations were written from my heart to yours. I am a person on a spiritual journey who has a growing relationship with God. I am not perfect nor am I claiming to be. I was once the believer who knew of God but did not know Him. I was once a believer who put people and things before God. 11 years later, I am a woman of God who still needs to be pruned, molded, and shaped to be more Christ like every day.

This spiritual walk has not always been easy, but it's a process I'm learning to endure to experience God miracles in my life. I pray that these conversations have helped you, encouraged you, renewed your faith, inspired you to want to change, and have given you the desire to want to know and understand God in a new way.

For weekly encouragement check out Brandi's Blog: praytheimpossible.com
For daily encouragement follow her on
Instagram @praytheimpossible
Facebook at facebook.com/praytheimpossible

AUTHOR'S BIO

Brandi J-E McAlister, MS is a New Jersey native. She obtained her BA in Mass Communications from Virginia State University. Later she completed her MS in Integrated Marketing Communication from Manhattanville College. Brandi is a dedicated member of Delta Sigma Theta Sorority, Incorporated.

As a woman of God, she loves encouraging, inspiring, and helping people has led her to her purpose in which she has titled, a Spiritual "Friendvisor." Brandi defines "Friendvisor" as a friend that gives advice based on Godly Wisdom.

Traveling, spending time with loved ones and dancing is what she enjoys most about life. Brandi's mantra is to Live, Love, Laugh and give all the glory to God.

REAL TALK

25535164R00063

Made in the USA
Columbia, SC
31 August 2018